Cambridge English

Starters 9

Answer Booklet

Cambridge University Press
www.cambridge.org/elt

Cambridge English Language Assessment
www.cambridgeenglish.org

Information on this title: www.cambridge.org/9781107464346

© Cambridge University Press and UCLES 2015

First published 2015
Reprinted 2016

Printed in Italy by Rotolito Lombarda S.p.A.

A catalogue record for this publication is available from the British Library

ISBN 978-1-107-46387-5 Student's Book
ISBN 978-1-107-46434-6 Answer Booklet
ISBN 978-1-107-46310-3 Audio CD

Contents

Introduction

The *Cambridge English: Young Learners* tests offer an elementary-level testing system (up to CEFR level A2) for learners of English between the ages of 7 and 12. The tests include three key levels of assessment: *Starters*, *Movers* and *Flyers*.

Starters is the lowest level in the system. Test instructions are very simple and consist only of words and structures specified in the syllabus.

The complete test lasts about 45 minutes and has the following components: Listening, Reading and Writing, and Speaking.

	length	number of parts	number of questions
Listening	approx. 20 minutes	4	20
Reading and Writing	20 minutes	5	25
Speaking	approx. 3–5 minutes	5	–

Candidates need a pen or pencil for the Reading and Writing paper, and coloured pens or pencils for the Listening paper. All answers are written on the question papers.

Listening

In general, the aim is to focus on the 'here and now' and to use language in meaningful contexts.
In addition to multiple-choice and short-answer questions, candidates are asked to use coloured pencils to mark their responses to one task. There are four parts. Each part begins with a clear example.

part	main skill focus	input	expected response	number of questions
1	listening for words and prepositions	picture and dialogue	carry out instructions and position things correctly on a picture	5
2	listening for numbers and spelling	illustrated comprehension questions and dialogue	write numbers and names	5
3	listening for specific information of various kinds	3-option multiple-choice pictures and dialogues	tick correct box under picture	5
4	listening for words, colours and prepositions	picture and dialogue	carry out instructions; locate objects and colour correctly (range of colours is: black, blue, brown, green, grey, orange, pink, purple, red, yellow)	5

Reading and Writing

Again, the focus is on the 'here and now' and the use of language in meaningful contexts where possible. To complete the test, candidates need a single pen or pencil of any colour. There are five parts, each starting with a clear example.

part	main skill focus	input	expected response	number of questions
1	reading short sentences and recognising words and sentences	words, pictures and sentences	tick or cross to show if sentence is true or false	5
2	reading sentences about a picture and writing one-word answers	picture and sentences	write 'yes'/ 'no'	5
3	spelling of single words	pictures and sets of jumbled letters	write words	5
4	reading a text and copying words	cloze text, words and pictures	choose and copy missing words	5
5	reading questions about a picture story and writing one-word answers	story presented through three pictures and questions	write one-word answers to questions	5

Speaking

In the Speaking test, the candidate speaks with one examiner for about four minutes. The format of the test is explained in advance to the child in their native language, by a teacher or person familiar to them. This person then takes the child into the exam room and introduces them to the examiner.

Speaking ability is assessed according to various criteria, including comprehension, the ability to produce an appropriate response and pronunciation.

part	main skill focus	input	expected response
1	understanding and following spoken instructions	scene picture	point to the correct part of the picture
2	understanding and following spoken instructions	scene picture and eight small object cards	place the object cards on the scene picture as directed
3	understanding and answering spoken questions	scene picture	answer questions with short answers
4	understanding and answering spoken questions	three object cards	answer questions with short answers
5	understanding and responding to personal questions	no visual prompt	answer questions with short answers

Further information

Further information about *Cambridge English: Young Learners* can be obtained from:

Cambridge English Language Assessment
1 Hills Road
Cambridge CB1 2EU
United Kingdom

www.cambridgeenglish.org/help
www.cambridgeenglish.org/younglearners

Test 1 Answers

Listening

Part 1 (5 marks)
Lines should be drawn between:
1 the shoe and under the dog
2 the coconut and between the woman and the duck
3 the doll and in the window
4 the mango and on the floor next to the boy
5 the glasses and the chicken's face

Part 2 (5 marks)
1 Lucy (correct spelling)   2 18/eighteen
3 Ben (correct spelling)   4 19/nineteen
5 3/three

Part 3 (5 marks)
1 A   2 C   3 B   4 C   5 C

Part 4 (5 marks)
1 Colour the bird with the baby – pink
2 Colour the bird flying between the boxes – red
3 Colour the bird behind the bike – orange
4 Colour the bird in the car – blue
5 Colour the bird next to the apples – yellow

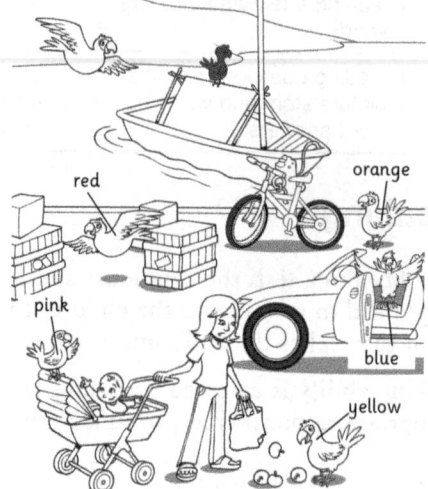

TRANSCRIPT   *Hello. This is the Cambridge English Starters Listening Test.*

Part 1   *Look at Part 1. Now look at the picture.*

Listen and look. There is one example.

[pause]

MAN: Look at the family in the garden.
WOMAN: Yes. I like their animals. Can I put the hat on the horse?
MAN: OK. Put the hat on the horse's head.

[pause]

Can you see the line? This is an example.

Now you listen and draw lines.

[pause]

1

WOMAN: What now?
MAN: Can you put the shoe under the dog?
WOMAN: Put the shoe where?
MAN: Under the dog, please.

[pause]

2

WOMAN: Where can I put the coconut?
MAN: Put it between the woman and the duck.
WOMAN: The coconut between the woman and the duck?
MAN: Yes, that's right.

[pause]

3

MAN: Can you see the doll?
WOMAN: Pardon?
MAN: The doll. Put it in the window.
WOMAN: OK. It's in the window now.

[pause]

4

MAN: Look. There's a mango.
WOMAN: Oh, yes. Can I put it next to the boy?
MAN: Yes. On the floor next to the boy, please.
WOMAN: OK. The mango's there now.

[pause]

5

WOMAN: Those are big glasses.
MAN: Yes, they are. Put them on the chicken's face.

WOMAN: Sorry, put the glasses where?
MAN: On the chicken's face. They look very nice!

[pause]

Now listen to Part 1 again.

[The recording is repeated.]

[pause]

That is the end of Part 1.

[pause]

Part 2   *Look at the picture. Listen and write a name or a number. There are two examples.*

[pause]

MAN: Hello. What's your name, please?
GIRL: It's Kim.
MAN: Do you spell Kim K-I-M?
GIRL: Yes, that's right.

[pause]

MAN: And how old are you, Kim?
GIRL: I'm nine. Today's my birthday!
MAN: Nine today? Happy birthday!
GIRL: Thank you.

[pause]

Can you see the answers?

Now you listen and write a name or a number.

[pause]

1

MAN: Is this your house?
GIRL: No, it isn't. It's my friend Lucy's house.
MAN: Lucy? How do you spell that?
GIRL: It's L-U-C-Y.
MAN: Right.

[pause]

2

MAN: Where's your house?
GIRL: It's in this street. It's number eighteen.
MAN: What number?
GIRL: Eighteen! It's there, look!
MAN: Oh, yes.

[pause]

3

MAN: And is that your cat?
GIRL: Yes, it is. His name's Ben.
MAN: Is that B-E-N?
GIRL: Yes.
MAN: Ben's a nice name for a cat.
GIRL: Thanks.

[pause]

4

MAN: Is your cat old?
GIRL: Yes, very old. He's nineteen.
MAN: How old is he?
GIRL: Nineteen.
MAN: That is old for a cat.

[pause]

5

MAN: Have you got lots of animals?
GIRL: Not lots, but I've got some lizards.
MAN: How many?
GIRL: I've got three.
MAN: Three lizards?
GIRL: Yes. But they haven't got names.

[pause]

Now listen to Part 2 again.

[The recording is repeated.]

[pause]

That is the end of Part 2.

[pause]

Part 3   *Look at the pictures. Now listen and look. There is one example.*

[pause]

What's in Bill's bedroom?

WOMAN: Have you got a mirror in your bedroom, Bill?
BOY: Yes, on my desk.
WOMAN: That's nice.
BOY: Yes, but I haven't got a lamp.

[pause]

Can you see the tick?

Now you listen and tick the box.

[pause]

1   *Where are the onions?*

WOMAN: Pat, I can't find the onions for dinner.
GIRL: Are they in the bag from the shop?
WOMAN: No, and they're not in the cupboard.
GIRL: Here they are, Mum. They're on the table!

[pause]

2   *What's Tom doing?*

GIRL: Tom's not playing soccer today.
BOY: I know. He's at his computer.
GIRL: Is he writing a story?
BOY: No. He's looking at a picture.

[pause]

3   *Which is Tony's mum?*

BOY: Look. There's my mum.
WOMAN: Is she wearing a T-shirt, Tony?

BOY: Yes, she is. And a hat.
WOMAN: Oh, yes. I like her handbag.

[pause]

4 What does Anna like doing on the beach?

BOY: Do you like fishing, Anna? There are lots of fish in the sea here.
GIRL: No. Look at the shells on the beach. I love picking them up.
BOY: I don't! Can we run?
GIRL: No. I don't like doing that.

[pause]

5 Where's the goat?

MAN: Sam, where's the goat?
BOY: In the garden, Dad.
MAN: Is it under the tree?
BOY: No … and it's not in front of the house. Oh no, it's in the flowers again!

[pause]

Now listen to Part 3 again.

[The recording is repeated.]

[pause]

That is the end of Part 3.

[pause]

Part 4   *Look at the picture. Listen and look. There is one example.*

[pause]

BOY: There are a lot of birds in this picture.
WOMAN: Yes, there are. Look at the bird on the boat.
BOY: Oh, yes. Can I colour it green?
WOMAN: OK. A green bird on the boat.

[pause]

Can you see the green bird on the boat?

This is an example.

Now you listen and colour.

[pause]

1

BOY: Oh, look! There's a bird with the baby!
WOMAN: Where?
BOY: There. It's sitting with the baby!
WOMAN: Oh, yes. Colour that bird pink.
BOY: Right. I'm colouring it pink now.

[pause]

2

BOY: And … there's a bird in the car.

WOMAN: Is there?
BOY: Yes. Can I colour the bird in the car blue?
WOMAN: Yes, that's good. Colour it blue.

[pause]

3

WOMAN: One bird's flying between the boxes.
BOY: What colour for that bird?
WOMAN: Red. Have you got a red pencil?
BOY: Yes, I have. I'm colouring the bird between the boxes now.
WOMAN: That's nice.

[pause]

4

BOY: Can I colour the bird behind the bike?
WOMAN: OK. What colour is that one? Orange?
BOY: Yes. That's a good colour.
WOMAN: Right. An orange bird behind the bike.

[pause]

5

BOY: Can you see the apples?
WOMAN: Yes. There's a bird next to them, too.
BOY: I'm colouring that bird yellow. Is that OK?
WOMAN: Yes. I like yellow.
BOY: And I like apples!

[pause]

Now listen to Part 4 again.

[The recording is repeated.]

[pause]

That is the end of the Starters Listening Test.

Reading and Writing

Part 1 (5 marks)
1 ✗   2 ✓   3 ✗   4 ✓   5 ✓

Part 2 (5 marks)
1 yes   2 no   3 yes   4 no   5 no

Part 3 (5 marks)
1 sofa   2 bath   3 radio   4 mirror
5 window

Part 4 (5 marks)
1 people   2 night   3 water   4 trees
5 playground

Part 5 (5 marks)
1 kite   2 kitchen   3 mum(my)/mother
4 painting   5 gran(d)dad/grandfather

Speaking

Part	Examiner does this:	Examiner says this:	Minimum response expected from child:	Back-up questions:
	Usher brings candidate in.	Usher to examiner: **Hello. This is (child's name*).** Examiner: **Hello, *. My name's** *Jane/Ms Smith.*	Hello.	
1	Points to **Scene** picture. Points to the girl in **Scene** picture.	**Look at this. This is a playroom. The children are playing table tennis.** **Here's the girl. *, where's the window? Where are the toys?**	Points to items in the picture.	**Is this the window? Are these the toys?**
2	Points to **Object** cards.	**Now look at these. Which is the clock?** **I'm putting the clock next to the ball.** **Now you put the clock under the table.** **Which is the ruler?** **Put the ruler behind the giraffe.** **Which is the camera/ boat?** **Put the camera/boat between the plane and the horse.**	Points to **Object** card. Puts **Object** card in place. Points to **Object** card. Puts **Object** card in place. Points to **Object** card. Puts **Object** card in place.	**Is this the clock?** (pointing to clock) **Where's the table?** <u>**Under**</u> **the table.** **Is this the ruler?** (pointing to ruler) **Where's the giraffe?** <u>**Behind**</u> **the giraffe.** **Is this the camera/boat?** (pointing to camera/boat) **Where are the plane and the horse?** <u>**Between**</u> **the plane and the horse.**
3	Removes **Object** cards and points to a flower in **Scene** picture. Points to the cat.	**Now, *, what's this? What colour is it?** **How many flowers are there?** **What's the cat doing?**	flower purple five sleeping	**Is it a flower? Is it orange? Purple?** **Are there four? Five?** **Is the cat sleeping?**

* Remember to use the child's name throughout the test.

Part	Examiner does this:	Examiner says this:	Minimum response expected from child:	Back-up questions:
4	Puts **Scene** picture away and picks out three **Object** cards.			
4.1	Shows **jacket** card.	What's this?	jacket	Is it a jacket?
		Are you wearing a jacket?	yes/no	
		What clothes do you wear at school?	jeans	Do you wear *jeans* at school?
4.2	Shows **mouse** card.	What's this?	mouse	Is it a mouse?
		Do you like mice?	yes/no	
		What's your favourite animal?	elephant	Do you like *elephants*?
4.3	Shows **eggs/bananas** card.	What are these?	eggs/bananas	Are they eggs/bananas?
		Do you eat eggs/ bananas?	yes/no	
		What do you eat for lunch?	chips/fries	Do you eat *chips/fries*?
5	Puts away all cards.	Now, *, how old are you?	10	Are you *10*?
		How many people are there in your family?	3	Are there *3* people in your family?
		Where do you watch television?	living room	Do you watch television in the *living room*?
		OK. Thank you, *. Goodbye.	Goodbye.	

* Remember to use the child's name throughout the test.

Test 2 Answers

Listening

Part 1 (5 marks)

Lines should be drawn between:

1 the lamp and in front of the window, on the floor
2 the painting and between the guitar and the board, on the wall
3 the eraser and in the box
4 the camera and between the computer and the book, on the table
5 the ruler and under the teacher's desk

Part 2 (5 marks)

1 Lucy (correct spelling)   2 12/twelve
3 Kim (correct spelling)   4 8/eight
5 Love (correct spelling)

Part 3 (5 marks)

1 A   2 C   3 A   4 B   5 A

Part 4 (5 marks)

1 Colour the hat of the boy in the tree – orange
2 Colour the hat of the girl playing in the water – blue
3 Colour the hat of the girl carrying fruit – yellow
4 Colour the hat of the girl drinking juice – pink
5 Colour the hat of the boy with the ice cream – brown

TRANSCRIPT   *Hello. This is the Cambridge English Starters Listening Test.*

Part 1   *Look at Part 1. Now look at the picture.*
Listen and look. There is one example.

[pause]

MAN: Look at the children in the classroom.
WOMAN: Yes. Can you see the doll?
MAN: Yes. Can I put it on the bookcase?
WOMAN: OK. Put the doll on the bookcase.

[pause]

Can you see the line? This is an example.

Now you listen and draw lines.

[pause]

1

MAN: Where can I put the lamp?
WOMAN: Let's see … Put it on the floor in front of the window.
MAN: On the floor in front of the window?
WOMAN: Yes. It's a very big lamp.

[pause]

2

MAN: That's a nice painting.
WOMAN: Yes, it is. Put it between the guitar and the board.
MAN: OK. I'm putting the painting between the guitar and the board now.
WOMAN: Well done.

[pause]

3

WOMAN: Now the eraser. Put it in the box.
MAN: In the box?
WOMAN: Yes.
MAN: Right. I'm putting the eraser there now.

[pause]

4

MAN: Can I put the camera between the computer and the book?
WOMAN: Sorry? Put the camera where?
MAN: Between the computer and the book.
WOMAN: Yes. That's good.

[pause]

5

MAN: Look! There's a ruler. Can I put it under the teacher's desk?
WOMAN: Put it under the teacher's desk?
MAN: Yes. The children can see the ruler, but the teacher can't see it.
WOMAN: Ha ha. OK.

Now listen to Part 1 again.

[The recording is repeated.]

That is the end of Part 1.

[pause]

Part 2 *Look at the picture. Listen and write a name or a number. There are two examples.*

[pause]

WOMAN: Hello. What's that?
GIRL: It's a photo for my friend. It's her birthday today.
WOMAN: That's good. What's her name?
GIRL: It's Anna.
WOMAN: Anna. Is that A-N-N-A?
GIRL: Yes.

[pause]

WOMAN: And how old is your friend today?
GIRL: She's fourteen.
WOMAN: Fourteen?
GIRL: That's right.

[pause]

Can you see the answers?

Now you listen and write a name or a number.

[pause]

1

WOMAN: Who's in the photo?
GIRL: Anna and her sister, Lucy.
WOMAN: Oh, yes. How do you spell Lucy?
GIRL: L-U-C-Y.

[pause]

2

WOMAN: And how old is Anna's sister?
GIRL: She's twelve.
WOMAN: Sorry?
GIRL: She's twelve.
WOMAN: Oh. OK.

[pause]

3

WOMAN: Have Anna and her sister got an animal in their house?
GIRL: Yes. Anna's got a funny mouse.
WOMAN: Has she?
GIRL: Yes. Its name's Kim.

WOMAN: Do you spell Kim K-I-M?
GIRL: Yes. It's black and white.

[pause]

4

GIRL: The mouse has got some babies.
WOMAN: Oh, great. How many?
GIRL: Eight.
WOMAN: Eight baby mice? That's a lot of babies!
GIRL: I know.

[pause]

5

WOMAN: And does Anna's family live in your street?
GIRL: No.
WOMAN: Where does her family live?
GIRL: In Love Street. That's L-O-V-E. Love Street.
WOMAN: Right.

Now listen to Part 2 again.

[The recording is repeated.]

That is the end of Part 2.

[pause]

Part 3 *Look at the pictures. Now listen and look. There is one example.*

[pause]

What are Bill and his dad playing?

WOMAN: Where's Bill? Is he playing tennis at school?
BOY: No. He's in the park with his dad.
WOMAN: Right. Are they playing baseball?
BOY: No, basketball. That's their favourite sport.

[pause]

Can you see the tick?

Now you listen and tick the box.

[pause]

1 Where's Mrs White's phone?

BOY: Can I phone my mum please, Mrs White?
WOMAN: Yes, Sam. The phone's on the sofa.
BOY: I can't find it.
WOMAN: Is it on the cupboard? Oh no, look! It's on the chair!

[pause]

2 What are Pat and her dad getting for lunch?

MAN: Let's get some chicken from this shop for lunch, Pat.
GIRL: I don't like that, Dad. Can we have fish?
MAN: They don't sell it here. Let's have eggs.
GIRL: OK.

[pause]

3 Which is Alex's toy?

GIRL: Is that your robot, Alex?
BOY: No. It's my brother's. That's my toy.
GIRL: Which one? The truck?
BOY: No. The train.

[pause]

4 What does Grandma like in May's picture?

WOMAN: Are you drawing a face, May?
GIRL: Yes, but I'm not very good. I can't draw eyes and noses.
WOMAN: Well, her mouth's very good. I like that a lot.
GIRL: Thanks, Grandma.

[pause]

5 What's behind the door?

GIRL: Look! What's that behind the door? I can see a tail.
BOY: What is it? A cat?
GIRL: No. It's a lizard!
BOY: Oh, great. It can say hello to my frog!
Now listen to Part 3 again.

[The recording is repeated.]

That is the end of Part 3.

[pause]

Part 4 *Look at the picture. Listen and look. There is one example.*

[pause]

BOY: Look at that big sun.
WOMAN: Yes. The children are wearing hats today.
BOY: One boy's got his hat on his face!
WOMAN: Oh, yes. He's sitting next to the bike. Colour his hat green.
BOY: OK. A green hat for that boy.

[pause]

Can you see the boy with a green hat? This is an example. Now you listen and colour.

[pause]

1

WOMAN: Can you see that boy? He's getting an apple from the tree.
BOY: Oh. I like apples.
WOMAN: Me too. Colour his hat orange.
BOY: Where's my orange pencil?
WOMAN: Here.
BOY: Oh, thanks.

[pause]

2

WOMAN: One girl's playing in the water.
BOY: Where?
WOMAN: There. Look!
BOY: Oh, yes. Can I colour her hat blue?

WOMAN: OK. A blue hat for the girl in the water.

[pause]

3

BOY: There's a lot of food.
WOMAN: Yes. And that girl's carrying a lot of fruit too.
BOY: Sorry?
WOMAN: Look, that girl there with fruit. Colour her hat yellow.
BOY: OK. I'm giving her a yellow hat now.

[pause]

4

WOMAN: Now look at that girl.
BOY: Which one?
WOMAN: That one. She's got a drink. Colour her hat pink.
BOY: Right. A pink hat for the girl with the drink.
WOMAN: Good.

[pause]

5

WOMAN: Who's your favourite person in the picture?
BOY: The boy with the ice cream. I love ice cream.
WOMAN: Me too. Colour his hat brown.
BOY: OK. I'm giving him a brown hat. I like this picture now!
Now listen to Part 4 again.

[The recording is repeated.]

[pause]

That is the end of the Starters Listening Test.

Reading and Writing

Part 1 (5 marks)
1 ✗   2 ✓   3 ✓   4 ✗   5 ✓

Part 2 (5 marks)
1 no   2 yes   3 no   4 yes   5 no

Part 3 (5 marks)
1 dress   2 jeans   3 skirt   4 jacket
5 trousers

Part 4 (5 marks)
1 family   2 bags   3 food   4 television/TV
5 books

Part 5 (5 marks)
1 yellow   2 monkey   3 elephant
4 boy/brother/kid/child
5 (small) (yellow) (tennis) ball

Speaking

Part	Examiner does this:	Examiner says this:	Minimum response expected from child:	Back-up questions:
	Usher brings candidate in.	Usher to examiner: **Hello. This is (child's name*).** Examiner: **Hello, *. My name's** *Jane/Ms Smith*.	**Hello.**	
1	Points to **Scene** picture.	**Look at this. This is a street. The woman's in front of the shop.**		
	Points to the hat in **Scene** picture.	**Here's the hat. *, where's the bird? Where are the oranges?**	Points to items in the picture.	**Is this the bird? Are these the oranges?**
2	Points to **Object** cards.	**Now look at these. Which is the chair?**	Points to **Object** card.	**Is this the chair?** (pointing to chair)
		I'm putting the chair under the bags.		
		Now you put the chair on the eggs.	Puts **Object** card in place.	**Where are the eggs? <u>On</u> the eggs.**
		Which are the glasses/ trousers?	Points to **Object** card.	**Are these the glasses/ trousers?** (pointing to glasses/ trousers)
		Put the glasses/trousers behind the cat.	Puts **Object** card in place.	**Where's the cat? <u>Behind</u> the cat.**
		Which is the handbag/ sock?	Points to **Object** card.	**Is this the handbag/ sock?** (pointing to handbag/ sock)
		Put the handbag/sock between the flowers and the mouse.	Puts **Object** card in place.	**Where are the flowers and the mouse? <u>Between</u> the flowers and the mouse.**
3	Removes **Object** cards and points to a banana in **Scene** picture.	**Now, *, what's this? What colour is it? How many bananas are there?**	banana yellow four	**Is it a banana? Is it pink? Yellow? Are there four? Five?**
	Points to the man.	**What's the man doing?**	riding (a bike)	**Is the man riding a bike?**

* Remember to use the child's name throughout the test.

Part	Examiner does this:	Examiner says this:	Minimum response expected from child:	Back-up questions:
4	Puts **Scene** picture away and picks out three **Object** cards.			
4.1	Shows **milk** card.	**What's this?** **Do you drink milk?** **What do you eat for breakfast?**	milk yes/no *bread*	Is it milk? Do you eat bread for breakfast?
4.2	Shows **house** card.	**What's this?** **Where do you live?** **Do you have a big bedroom?**	house (name of town or city) yes/no	Is it a house? Do you live in (name of town or city)? Is your bedroom big?
4.3	Shows **piano** card.	**What's this?** **Can you play the piano?** **What colour is your/this piano?**	piano yes/no *white*	Is it a piano? Is your/this piano *white*?
5	Puts away all cards.	**Now, *, how many people are there in your family?** **Is your teacher a man or a woman?** **Where do you go with your friends?**	*4* *man* *park*	Are there *four* people in your family? Is your teacher a *man*? Do you go to the *park* with your friends?
		OK. Thank you, *. **Goodbye.**	 **Goodbye.**	

* Remember to use the child's name throughout the test.

Test 3 Answers

Listening

Part 1 (5 marks)

Lines should be drawn between:

1 the lamp and under the fish
2 the snake and on the chair
3 the glasses and between the shoe and the box
4 the lizard and in the bath
5 the hat and on the man's head

Part 2 (5 marks)

1 Sun (correct spelling)   2 3/three
3 Page (correct spelling)   4 12/twelve
5 Tom (correct spelling)

Part 3 (5 marks)

1 A   2 B   3 C   4 B   5 C

Part 4 (5 marks)

1 Colour the duck next to the kite – blue
2 Colour the duck on the horse – purple
3 Colour the duck in the girl's hand – orange
4 Colour the duck in the box – green
5 Colour the duck behind the ball – red

TRANSCRIPT   *Hello. This is the Cambridge English Starters Listening Test.*

Part 1   *Look at Part 1. Now look at the picture. Listen and look. There is one example.*

[pause]

WOMAN: I like the small frog.
MAN: Yes. Can you put it on the flower?
WOMAN: OK. I'm putting the frog on the flower.
MAN: Thank you!

[pause]

Can you see the line? This is an example. Now you listen and draw lines.

[pause]

1

MAN: Can you see the lamp?
WOMAN: Yes. I can see it.
MAN: Put it under the fish.
WOMAN: The lamp under the fish? OK.

[pause]

2

MAN: Now, put the snake on the chair.
WOMAN: Put the snake on the chair?
MAN: Yes. That's right.
WOMAN: I'm doing that now.

[pause]

3

WOMAN: What can I do now?
MAN: Can you see the glasses?
WOMAN: Yes. Can I put them between the shoe and the box?
MAN: Yes. Put the glasses between the shoe and the box.

[pause]

4

MAN: Now find the lizard.
WOMAN: Can I put it in the bath?
MAN: Yes. Very good. Put the lizard in the bath.
WOMAN: OK.

[pause]

5

MAN:	And can you see the hat?
WOMAN:	Yes.
MAN:	Put it on the man's head.
WOMAN:	Right. I'm putting the hat on the man's head now.

[pause]

Now listen to Part 1 again.

[The recording is repeated.]

[pause]

That is the end of Part 1.

[pause]

Part 2 *Look at the picture. Listen and write a name or a number. There are two examples.*

[pause]

WOMAN:	What's your name?
BOY:	It's Alex Wall.
WOMAN:	Can you spell Wall for me?
BOY:	Yes. It's W-A-L-L.
WOMAN:	Thank you.

[pause]

WOMAN:	How old are you, Alex?
BOY:	I'm eight.
WOMAN:	Eight?
BOY:	Yes.

[pause]

Can you see the answers? Now you listen and write a name or a number.

[pause]

1

WOMAN:	Where do you live, Alex?
BOY:	I live at number 15, Sun Street.
WOMAN:	Can you spell Sun for me?
BOY:	Yes. It's S-U-N.
WOMAN:	Thank you.

[pause]

2

WOMAN:	Which class are you in at school?
BOY:	I'm in class three.
WOMAN:	Which class?
BOY:	Class three.

[pause]

3

WOMAN:	What's your teacher's name?
BOY:	Her name's Mrs Page.
WOMAN:	How do you spell Page?
BOY:	You spell it P-A-G-E.
WOMAN:	Thank you.

[pause]

4

WOMAN:	Do you like reading?
BOY:	Yes. I read a lot of books.
WOMAN:	How many books have you got today?
BOY:	Twelve.
WOMAN:	Twelve books? That is a lot.

[pause]

5

WOMAN:	Do you have a favourite book?
BOY:	Yes, I do. It's *Cousin Tom*.
WOMAN:	I don't know that story. Do you spell Tom, T-O-M?
BOY:	That's right.
WOMAN:	OK. Thank you, Alex.

[pause]

Now listen to Part 2 again.

[The recording is repeated.]

[pause]

That is the end of Part 2.

[pause]

Part 3 *Look at the pictures. Now listen and look. There is one example.*

[pause]

What's Nick's favourite food?

WOMAN:	Are you eating your favourite food, Nick?
BOY:	No, that's fish. But I like chicken too.
WOMAN:	What about burgers?
BOY:	They're OK.

[pause]

Can you see the tick? Now you listen and tick the box.

[pause]

1 What's on the table?

BOY:	I can't find my school bag.
WOMAN:	Er, it's on your bed. Your watch is there too.
BOY:	What about my pencils?
WOMAN:	They're on the kitchen table.

[pause]

2 Which ice cream is Lucy eating?

MAN:	Are you eating banana ice cream, Lucy?
GIRL:	No, I don't like that. This is mango.
MAN:	I like pineapple ice cream.
GIRL:	Me, too.

[pause]

3 Where is Anna's grandma?

WOMAN:	Where's Grandma? Is she watching TV in the living room, Anna?
GIRL:	No, she isn't.

WOMAN: Is she making lunch in the kitchen?
GIRL: No, she isn't. She's sleeping on her bed.

[pause]

4 What can Sam's brother do?

WOMAN: Can your baby brother talk, Sam?
BOY: No, he's too young.
WOMAN: Can he walk?
BOY: Yes, but he can't run.

[pause]

5 What's Kim drawing?

WOMAN: I like your picture, Kim. Is that an elephant?
BOY: No. It hasn't got big ears.
WOMAN: It's got a very big mouth. Is it a hippo?
BOY: No, it's a cow. Look!

[pause]

Now listen to Part 3 again.

[The recording is repeated.]

[pause]

That is the end of Part 3.

[pause]

Part 4 Look at the picture. Listen and look. There is one example.

[pause]

MAN: Can you see the duck on the water?
GIRL: Yes.
MAN: Can you colour it yellow?
GIRL: Colour the duck on the water yellow?
MAN: Yes, please.

[pause]

Can you see the yellow duck on the water? This is an example. Now you listen and colour.

[pause]

1

MAN: Now find the duck next to the kite.
GIRL: Which duck?
MAN: The duck next to the kite. Please colour it blue.
GIRL: Blue. OK. I can do that.
MAN: Good.

[pause]

2

MAN: There's a duck on the horse.
GIRL: Yes, I can see the duck on the horse.
MAN: Can you colour it purple, please?
GIRL: A purple duck! OK.

[pause]

3

MAN: Now can you colour the duck in the girl's hand?
GIRL: What colour do you want?
MAN: Orange, please.
GIRL: Colour the duck in the girl's hand orange. Right.

[pause]

4

MAN: What about the duck in the box?
GIRL: Can I colour it green?
MAN: OK.
GIRL: Right. I'm colouring the duck in the box green.

[pause]

5

MAN: Can you see the duck behind the dog's ball?
GIRL: Yes.
MAN: Can you colour the duck behind the dog's ball red?
GIRL: Colour it red. OK.
MAN: That's a nice picture now.

[pause]

Now listen to Part 4 again.

[The recording is repeated.]

[pause]

That is the end of the Starters Listening Test.

Reading and Writing

Part 1 (5 marks)
1 ✗   2 ✓   3 ✗   4 ✓   5 ✓

Part 2 (5 marks)
1 no   2 yes   3 yes   4 yes   5 no

Part 3 (5 marks)
1 desk   2 ruler   3 eraser   4 bookcase
5 computer

Part 4 (5 marks)
1 family   2 school   3 arms   4 toys
5 milk

Part 5 (5 marks)
1 (large/big) (grandfather) clock   2 cat
3 flying/singing   4 (top of the) (living room) door
5 girl/child/kid/daughter/sister

Speaking

Part	Examiner does this:	Examiner says this:	Minimum response expected from child:	Back-up questions:
	Usher brings candidate in.	Usher to examiner: **Hello. This is (child's name*).**		
		Examiner: **Hello, *.** My name's *Jane/Ms Smith*.	Hello.	
1	Points to **Scene** picture.	**Look at this. This is a park. It's a nice day.**		
	Points to the dog in **Scene** picture.	**Here's the dog. *, where's the bird? Where are the bikes?**	Points to items in the picture.	**Is this the bird? Are these the bikes?**
2	Points to **Object** cards.	**Now look at these. Which is the car?**	Points to **Object** card.	**Is this the car?** (pointing to car)
		I'm putting the car behind the girl.		
		Now you put the car next to the bag.	Puts **Object** card in place.	**Where's the bag?** <u>Next to</u> **the bag.**
		Which is the robot/ shell?	Points to **Object** card.	**Is this the robot/shell?** (pointing to robot/shell)
		Put the robot/shell in the water.	Puts **Object** card in place.	**Where's the water?** <u>In</u> **the water.**
		Which is the phone/ radio?	Points to **Object** card.	**Is this the phone/radio?** (pointing to phone/radio)
		Put the phone/radio on the boy.	Puts **Object** card in place.	**Where's the boy?** <u>On</u> **the boy.**
3	Removes **Object** cards and points to the blue flower in **Scene** picture.	**Now, *, what's this? What colour is it? How many flowers are there?**	flower blue five	**Is it a flower? Is it orange? Blue? Are there four? Five?**
	Point to the fish.	**What are the fish doing?**	swimming	**Are the fish swimming?**
4	Puts **Scene** picture away and picks out three **Object** cards.			
4.1	Shows **watermelon** card.	**What's this? Do you like watermelon? What's your favourite fruit?**	watermelon yes/no *grapes*	**Is it a watermelon?** **Do you like *grapes*?**
4.2	Shows **shoes** card.	**What are these? Are your shoes clean or dirty? What colour are your shoes?**	shoes *clean* red	**Are they shoes? Are your shoes *clean*?** **Are they *red*?**
4.3	Shows **television** card.	**What's this? Do you like watching television? Where is the television in your house?**	TV/television yes/no *living room*	**Is it a TV/television?** **Is there a television in your *living room*?**

* Remember to use the child's name throughout the test.

Part	Examiner does this:	Examiner says this:	Minimum response expected from child:	Back-up questions:
5	Puts away all cards.	Now, *, is your school big or small?	*small*	Is your school *small*?
		What's your friend's name?	*(friend's name)*	Is your friend's name ...?
		What sport do you play at school?	*basketball*	Do you play *basketball* at your school?
		OK. Thank you, *.		
		Goodbye.	Goodbye.	

* Remember to use the child's name throughout the test.

STARTERS THEMATIC VOCABULARY LIST

For ease of reference, vocabulary is arranged in semantic groups or themes. Some words appear under more than one heading.

In addition to the topics, notions and concepts listed for the syllabus, the following categories appear:

- useful words and expressions
- adjectives
- determiners
- adverbs
- prepositions
- conjunctions
- pronouns
- verbs
- modals
- question words
- names

ANIMALS

animal
bird
cat
chicken
cow
crocodile
dog
duck
elephant
fish (s & pl)
frog
giraffe
goat
hippo
horse
lizard
monkey
mouse/mice
sheep (s & pl)
snake
spider
tail
tiger
zoo

THE BODY & FACE

arm
body
ear
eye
face
foot/feet
hair
hand
head
leg
mouth
nose
smile

CLOTHES

bag
clothes
dress
glasses
handbag
hat
jacket
jeans
shirt
shoe
skirt
sock
trousers
T-shirt
watch
wear

COLOURS

black
blue
brown
green
grey (or gray)
orange
pink
purple
red
white
yellow

FAMILY & FRIENDS

baby
boy
brother
child/children
cousin
dad(dy)
family
father
friend
girl
grandfather
grandma
grandmother
grandpa
live
man/men
Miss
mother
Mr
Mrs
mum(my) (US mom(my))
old
person/people
sister
their
them
they
us
we
woman/women
you
young
your

FOOD & DRINK

apple
banana
bean
bread
breakfast
burger
cake
carrot
chicken
chips (US fries)
coconut
dinner

drink (n & v)
eat
egg
fish
food
fries (UK chips)
fruit
grape
ice cream
juice
lemon
lemonade
lime
lunch
mango
meat
milk
onion
orange
pea
pear
pineapple
potato
rice
sausage
supper
tomato
water
watermelon

THE HOME

apartment
armchair
bath
bathroom
bed
bedroom
bookcase
box
camera
chair
clock
computer
cupboard
desk
dining room
doll
door
flat
floor
flower
garden
hall
house
kitchen
lamp
living room
mat
mirror
painting
phone
picture

radio
room
sleep
sofa
table
television/TV
toy
tree
wall
watch
window

NUMBERS

Cardinals: 1–20

PLACES & DIRECTIONS

behind
between
here
in
in front of
next to
on
park
shop (US store)
store (UK shop)
street
there
under
zoo

SCHOOL

alphabet
answer
ask
board
book
bookcase
class
classroom
close
colour
computer
correct
cross
cupboard
desk
door
draw(ing)
English
eraser
example
find
floor
know
learn
lesson
letter (as in alphabet)
line
listen (to)
look

name
number
open
page
part
pen
pencil
picture
playground
question
read
right (as in correct)
rubber
ruler
school
sentence
spell
stand (up)
story
teacher
tell
test (n & v)
tick (n & v)
understand
wall
window
word
write

SPORTS & LEISURE

badminton
ball
baseball
basketball
beach
bike
boat
book
bounce
camera
catch
doll
draw(ing)
drive (v)
enjoy
favourite
fish(ing)
fly
football (US soccer)
game
guitar
hit
hobby
hockey
jump
kick (v)
kite
listen (to)
paint(ing)
photo
piano
picture

play (with)
radio
read
ride (v)
run
sing
soccer (UK football)
song
sport
story
table tennis
television/TV
tennis
throw
toy
TV/television
watch

TIME

afternoon
birthday
clock
day
end
evening
morning
night
today
watch
year

TOYS

alien
ball
balloon
baseball
basketball
bike
boat
car
doll
football
game
helicopter
kite
lorry (US truck)
monster
plane
robot
toy
train
truck (UK lorry)

TRANSPORT

bike
boat
bus
car
drive (v)
fly (v)
go

helicopter
lorry (US truck)
motorbike
plane
ride (v)
run
swim
train
truck (UK lorry)

WEATHER

sun

WORK

teacher

THE WORLD AROUND US

beach
sand
sea
shell
street
sun
tree
water

USEFUL WORDS & EXPRESSIONS

bye (-bye)
goodbye
hello
I don't know
no
oh
oh dear
OK
pardon
please
right
so
sorry
thank you
thanks
then
well
well done
wow!
yes

ADJECTIVES

angry
beautiful
big
clean
closed
correct
dirty
double
English
favourite

funny
good
great
happy
her
his
its
long
my
new
nice
old
open
our
right (correct)
sad
short
small
sorry
their
ugly
young
your

DETERMINERS

a/an
a lot of
lots of
many
my
no
one
some
that
the
these
this
those

ADVERBS

a lot
again
here
lots
no
not
now
really
then
there
today
too
very
yes

PREPOSITIONS

about
at (prep of place)
behind
between
for

from
in (prep of place)
in front of
like
next to
of
on
to
under
with

CONJUNCTIONS

and
but
or

PRONOUNS

he
her
hers
him
his
I
it
its
me
mine
one
ours
she
that
theirs
them
these
they
this
those
us
we
you
yours

VERBS

Irregular:
be
catch (a ball)
choose
come
do
draw
drink

drive
eat
find
fly
get
give
go
have
have (got)
hit
hold
know
learn
let's
make
put
read
ride
run
say
see
sing
sit (down)
sleep
spell
stand (up)
swim
take (a photo)
tell
throw
understand
wear
write

Regular:
add
answer
ask
bounce
clean
close
colour
complete
cross
enjoy
jump
kick
learn
like
listen (to)
live
look
look at

love
open
paint
phone
pick up
play (with)
point
show
smile
start
stop
talk
test
tick
try
walk
want
watch
wave

MODALS

can/cannot/can't

QUESTION WORDS

how
how many
how old
what
where
which
who
whose

NAMES

Alex
Ann
Anna
Ben
Bill
Dan
Grace
Jill
Kim
Lucy
May
Nick
Pat
Sam
Sue
Tom
Tony